THE

GHOSTLY TALES

OF

BARABOO

Published by Arcadia Children's Books
A Division of Arcadia Publishing
Charleston, SC
www.arcadiapublishing.com

Spooky America is a trademark of Arcadia Publishing, Inc.

First published 2022

Manufactured in the United States

ISBN 978-1-4671-9862-2

Library of Congress Control Number: 2022932231

Notice: The information in this book is true and complete to the best of our knowledge. It is offered without guarantee on the part of the author or Arcadia Publishing. The author and Arcadia Publishing disclaim all liability in connection with the use of this book.

All images courtesy of Shutterstock

Spooky America

THE
GHOSTLY TALES
OF
BARABOO

ANNA LARDINOIS

Adapted from *Haunted Baraboo* by Shelley Mordini and Gwen Herrewig

arcadia
CHILDREN'S BOOKS

TABLE OF CONTENTS

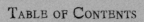

Introduction

Welcome to spook-tacular BaraBOO! Baraboo might not be a big town, but it has some very big-name ghosts! A few of Wisconsin's most famous ghosts are lurking in Baraboo. For example, the Old Baraboo Inn on Walnut Street is considered to be one of the most haunted buildings in the state of Wisconsin. Curious ghost fans from across the country visit the building in hopes of having an eerie encounter with the spirits that have made the former inn their home.

Another famous, and famously frightening, ghost in Baraboo is the mysterious Highway 12 hitchhiker! People drive long distances just to reach the lonely stretch of highway where this apparition appears. He has terrified generations of drivers who got more than they bargained for in their search of this roaming spirit.

It's not just ghosts that bring visitors to Baraboo. It's often called "Circus City" because seven circuses claim roots in Baraboo, and fans of the circus from all over the world visit to learn about the history of the circus. One of the most well-known circuses is the Ringling Brothers, started by brothers Al., Alf T., Otto, Charles, and John Ringling in May 1884. In time, the Ringling Brothers circus grew to be one of the largest and most famous circuses in the entire world!

Back in those days, when the weather was warm, the circus would travel all over the country, but when it got cold, the Ringling brothers would come home to Baraboo to spend the winter. When they came home, they brought the circus with them. It might be hard to believe, but at one time, it was as common to see an elephant, a zebra, or a camel taking a walk in Baraboo like any other pet!

Nowadays, circus fans love to visit Circus World Museum and the buildings that were connected to the famous Ringling brothers. And a surprising number of those buildings are reported to be haunted!

It seems that circus people must have liked Baraboo very much, because legend has it that quite a few people involved in the Ringling Brothers circus remain in the city, long after their deaths.

These spooky specters carry on just as they did when they were alive, haunting the homes, theaters, and visitor shops they once occupied in life. These spirits do all sorts of things around

Baraboo that you and I do every day, except these residents died a long time ago!

What is it about Baraboo that makes it so haunted? We are not sure, but we do know there is plenty of BOO! in Baraboo. Turn the page to meet some of the spine-tingling specters that still linger in this town.

Read on—if you dare!

The Old Baraboo Inn

Did you know that one of Wisconsin's most haunted buildings is right in downtown Baraboo? It's true! People come from all over the state in hopes of catching a glimpse of one of the spooky spirits that are reported to linger at the Old Baraboo Inn. This place is so well known that it has been on the Food Network's 10 Most Haunted Restaurants in America and the Travel Channel's Hometown Horror.

B.C. Farr, the owner of the Old Baraboo Inn, has had more than his fair share of paranormal experiences in the building. The spirits that reside there made themselves known to him shortly after he purchased the building in 2001. At first, small things happened. He noticed his tools were being moved by an unseen hand. Lights would inexplicably turn themselves on in the middle of the night. Occasionally, he'd even hear someone call out his name from inside the empty building. Spooky, right? Turns out, that

was just the start of things. Before long, the spirits got MUCH bolder!

One day, B.C. heard a glass shatter in the kitchen. He was surprised by the sound because no one was working in the kitchen at the time. When he poked his head into the room to investigate, he was in for the shock of his life! He saw plates flying through the air! He watched in disbelief as plates were thrown across the room by an unseen hand. Each of the plates smashed into pieces when it hit the kitchen wall. Shaken,

B.C. called out into the seemingly empty room that plates were expensive. Not knowing what to do, he left the kitchen and closed the door.

Soon, the sounds of breaking dishes stopped, and the empty kitchen was silent. When B.C. gathered the courage to open the kitchen door, he found broken dishes all over the floor. Frustrated, he shouted, "Well, this is a fine mess! Who is going to clean this up?" Within moments, a broom flew from a cabinet. It scooted around the kitchen floor as if being pushed by an invisible being. The broom swept itself across the room, gathering the shards of broken dishes. In disbelief, B.C. watched as the broom deposited the pile of broken dishes at his feet. How could that possibly happen? It HAD to be a ghost!

Not all of the spirits in the building are unseen. The ghost of a tall man wearing a brown cowboy hat has been spotted in the Old Baraboo Inn over the years. Additionally, in the back room of the building, there appears to be a group of ghostly children who like to play with the living children who visit the inn. Shocked parents have reported seeing their kids holding hands with these specters.

The ghostly children are thought to play pranks in the ladies' room of the inn. These spooky kids will cause the toilets to flush, and people using the bathroom have seen the lid of the garbage can soar across the room on its own. Once, a mischievous ghost even placed the whole trash can in a bathroom stall while a very unlucky lady was using the toilet. Talk about an unexpected surprise!

The most famous spirit that calls the Old Baraboo Inn home is the ghost who people call Mary. She has been seen for decades twirling across the dance floor in a short red dress with a feather tucked into her long, blonde hair. Mary is most often spotted when the song "The House

is Rockin'" by Stevie Ray Vaughn is played on the jukebox.

People from all over come to the Old Baraboo Inn and feed their money into the jukebox, pressing the numbers to play ghostly Mary's favorite song. So, what's the connection between the spirit of a woman who supposedly died in the building in 1903 and a song that was recorded in 1989? If Mary did die in 1903, it might be the reason why this ghost will appear when the numbers 1-9-0-3 are selected on the jukebox.

According to B.C., most of the spooky specters that remain at the Old Baraboo Inn seem to enjoy interacting with visitors and staff. But there are a few who seem a little less than friendly.

One of those spirits can be found in the basement of the building. Visitors to this legendary basement go down a flight of narrow, wooden stairs to reach a dark collection of small rooms with dirt floors. Some say the basement was once a place where illegal activities occurred, but no one knows for sure what exactly happened in these gloomy rooms below the inn. One thing people do seem to know is the spirit that lingers in the dark basement will sometimes play mean tricks on people who enter its space.

More than one staff member has gone down to the basement to get items from a walk-in cooler, only to find themselves trapped! As the person enters the refrigerated room, the door closes, and suddenly, the lights go out. Plunged into darkness, the person will reach out to open the door, only to find it locked! Being locked inside the cold, dark freezer is a frigid and frightening experience that none of the staff are eager to have happen again.

Fortunately, not everything that happens in the basement is scary. Once an employee was carrying a heavy box up the basement steps and lost her balance. Instead of tumbling down the stairs, the employee felt a presence behind her. An unseen hand steadied the employee and

managed to avoid an accident. That is one helpful ghost!

Those looking to have their own ghostly experience can check into the haunted room available for rent on the second floor of the inn. But beware! Staying the night in this two-bedroom suite is strictly for the brave. One adventure-seeker got more than he bargained for after spending the night in the reportedly haunted room.

The man was sitting in a chair and realized he was growing sleepy. He decided it was time for him to head to bed. As he stood up, he felt a strange pressure on his chest. He looked down, but nothing was touching him. The strange sensation stopped him in his tracks. And he is glad that it did!

Within moments, the light fixture above him came falling down from the ceiling! Sparks flew as the fixture crashed to the floor, barely missing the man's head! The strange "accident" overwhelmed the electrical circuit, which caused the electricity to shut off in the room. The man was terrified as he stood in the pitch dark. Not waiting to see what would happen next, the man ran out of the room without looking back!

The employees of the Old Baraboo Inn received a frantic phone call from the man at one in the morning. He was calling from the sidewalk in front of the building because he was far too frightened to return to the haunted suite. Understandably so! Unfortunately for him, he had no choice but to go back to the eerie room if he wanted to sleep indoors. He was told there were no other rooms available in Baraboo that night. He reluctantly returned, but I bet he didn't sleep very soundly!

B.C. has one important warning for

non-believers who visit the Old Baraboo Inn: if you don't believe in ghosts, you may want to keep that information to yourself. The ghosts who have made the building their home often show non-believers just how real they are. B.C. calls the practice getting "ghost bombed." These spooky specters have been changing people's minds about the existence of ghosts for decades.

So, what do you think? Are you brave enough to experience this famously haunted building for yourself? Your own spooky adventure could be just a visit away!

Two Scoops of Spooky

Have you ever heard the saying, "I scream, you scream, we all scream for ice cream?" Well, at the Tin Roof Dairy on Third Avenue, there might be more to scream over than just ice cream!

Legend has it that the building, constructed in 1872, is haunted. It's been many different things over the years, but in 2019, it became an ice-cream parlor, Tin Roof Dairy. Since then, there have been a number of strange occurrences inside the shop.

The owner of the Tin Roof Dairy, Michael Yount, is a skeptical man. He is not certain that anything paranormal is happening in his shop. But he's had a few strange experiences that have made him wonder if ghosts really do exist. Read on, and decide for yourself: Are these unexplained events proof that there is something supernatural in the building?

When the shop first opened, Michael put bells above the door to let the staff know when customers enter the parlor. The bells ring every time someone opens the door, so they hear them jingle all day every day.

But, about twice a week, something strange happens. The bells ring on their own. Yes, you read that right—the bells will ring, even though there is no one near the door. Nobody in the shop could understand how it was happening. Michael decided to get to the bottom of the mysterious ringing, so he began to conduct experiments.

At first, he thought the bells might be stuck. They weren't. Then he thought the wind might be blowing on the bells and causing them to ring. That wasn't it either. He bumped the door, but still, no bells. He tried everything he could think of to get those bells to ring without opening the door. But he just couldn't make it happen.

Michael still didn't think bells ringing on their own was evidence that a ghost was lurking in the ice-cream parlor, but he certainly thought the ringing was puzzling.

The strange events didn't stop there. One

time, while working in the back room, Michael heard footsteps on the roof of the building. There is only one way to get to the roof. A person would have to go through an apartment on the upper floor of the building, but the apartment was vacant and the door to the apartment was locked. No one could be up there . . . or could they?

He didn't just hear the footsteps on the roof once. Not even twice! He heard someone walking across the roof THREE different times! After the third time, he raced up the stairs to investigate. He found the door to the apartment was still locked, and the apartment was still vacant. He couldn't figure out who—or what—was walking across the roof that day. Michael doesn't think it is a ghost, but what else could it be?

Perhaps the eeriest event of all involves a small musical carousel that sits on a shelf in the ice-cream parlor. No one had played with the musical carousel in a while, so it had not been wound up in a very long time. Suddenly, it started to play on its own. The horse on top of the base began to spin, and the tinny-sounding music that was being plucked out by the music box filled the room.

At first, no one was certain where the music was coming from. A few people inside the shop checked their phones, thinking the sound might be a ring tone. Moments later, they spotted the carousel moving without any earthly assistance. Then, just as suddenly as it began, the musical carousel shut itself off. What else could explain this besides ghostly meddling?

Do you agree with Michael? Are these just a series of strange events that mean nothing? Or do you agree with some of the employees at the ice-cream parlor that

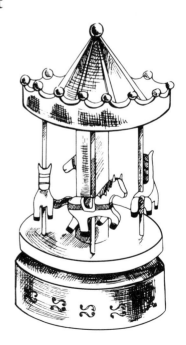

all of these otherworldly happenings are proof that a phantom is in the building?

I think the Tin Roof Dairy might be the best place in the world to do some of your own ghost hunting. Grab an ice cream cone and do a little investigating. Just remember, you shouldn't assume that cold chill you feel inside the shop is from the freezers where all of that delicious ice cream is stored. It very well could be a spectral presence who is nearer than you think!

Frightful Footsteps in the Van Orden Mansion

Carl Smith worked at the Van Orden mansion on Fourth Avenue in Baraboo for nine years. If you ask him, there is no doubt about it: the building is definitely haunted. And the mystery that needs to be unraveled is the identity of the ghostly spirit that still lingers there.

The strange tale of this house begins with Jacob Van Orden. He moved to Baraboo in 1874, when he was just eighteen years old. He got a job at a bank and was responsible for running errands and keeping the bank clean. But Jacob worked hard, and within five years, he was promoted to the job of teller. In 1885, he gave the Ringling brothers a $100 loan to start their circus. The circus was a success, and in time, the Ringlings became one of the bank's biggest clients.

All of his hard work made Jacob a wealthy man. So, he decided it was time to build the home of his dreams. In 1903, Jacob Van Orden, his wife, Martha, and their two children walked through their newly completed, fourteen-room home for the first time. His mansion had every modern convenience of the time, including electric lighting and indoor plumbing! With five fireplaces, marble sinks, and

a third-floor ballroom, it was among the most luxurious homes in all of Baraboo.

Jacob died in 1927 at the age of seventy-one. Martha joined him on the other side in 1832. After that, their son, Lucas, lived in the home with his wife, Florence. The Van Orden family left the home in 1938, but their legacy lives on. Today, Jacob Van Orden's beloved home is the location of the Sauk County Historic Museum.

While the Van Orden family may no longer live in the home, it does seem that something or someone from their time there still lingers. At least that's what many people believe. And by the end of this story, you just might think so, too.

Carl and his coworkers would often report hearing the sounds of someone moving around when they thought they were alone in the home. From his first-floor desk, Carl heard the footsteps of someone strolling through the upper floors of the home. Sometimes the footsteps could be heard from the second floor, and other times, he could hear the tread of feet coming from the attic. The unseen presence seemed to always be moving on the floor above wherever Carl was in the home.

Even stranger was that when Carl knew someone was working on the second floor, he NEVER heard that person walking on the stairs or in the hallways. The employees tried many things, but they could not replicate the sounds of footsteps walking overhead. As unbelievable as it was, a ghost seemed to be the only explanation for the disembodied footsteps!

It isn't just the disembodied footsteps echoing in the empty building that make people think the Van Orden Mansion is haunted. Carl reported that about once a month, a loud crash could be heard throughout the home. Employees would search high and low for the source of the clatter, but nothing could be found. Each time the bone-rattling sound was heard, the staff would go from room to room, looking to see if a picture

had fallen off the wall, or a heavy book tumbled to the floor—anything to explain the noise. Despite their many searches, to this day, no one has found an explanation for the crashes. Could they be more evidence that something lurks in the home?

It's not only the people who work at the Van Orden mansion who believe it is haunted. A few unlucky people who have walked by the home at night have reason to think something lurks there. More than one late-night passerby has reported the curtains in an upper floor window moving as if someone is peering between the folds of cloth. This might not be so unusual if it didn't happen long after the museum was closed for the night—and in a place where it is impossible for a living being to reach those curtains! It seems the curtains are always disturbed in a room where the window is surrounded by a large display case. A person would have to be able to move through furniture to get to the window. Which is impossible, right? If it isn't a ghost, just what could it be peeking from the upstairs window?

Just who is the ghostly presence that lingers in this historic building? Some think the spirit that walks through the house at night is Viola Putz. Viola came to the home when she was nineteen to work as a maid for Lucas and Florence. Viola had been a maid in the home for nine years when she suddenly grew sick in the summer of 1937. The illness did not seem serious. At least, not at first. But Viola became very ill very quickly, and she was taken to the hospital. She died just two days later at the age of twenty-eight. The unexpected death shocked the town. Soon, townspeople began to gossip about Viola's death. They had suspicions about how a young, healthy woman could die so quickly. Despite the rumors, nothing strange was ever reported about the death of the young maid.

No one truly knows if Viola is the spirit who still walks the halls of the Van Orden mansion. If she does still roam the home, why does she remain? Does it have something to do with her untimely death?

The next time you are passing by the old Van Orden mansion, take a look at the upper windows and see if you catch a glimpse of someone looking back at you. Maybe you will be able to identify who is peeking out of the curtains and finally solve the mystery of just who haunts this famous home.

The Fighting Spirits of Boo-U

The University of Wisconsin-Platteville at Baraboo Sauk County is known as "Boo-U." The name is a fun take on its location in Baraboo and has nothing to do with the possibility that the campus is haunted. Or does it? The school mascot is a ghost, so there must be something spooky going on, right? A couple of former students who spent time behind the scenes in the theater department say that's exactly what is going on at Boo-U.

Drake Lewerenz and Rebecca Hassebrock, two former assistants to the theater director, had eerie experiences when they worked in the theater department. The activity seemed to center around the costume area under the stage. They discovered that the school mascot is not the only ghost on campus!

One day back in 2012, Drake was alone in the costume room tidying up. He was busy folding bolts of fabric when he suddenly noticed a chilling silence descend on the room. He paused for a moment and then heard a strange sound coming from the nearby boiler room. He listened intently, trying to identify the sound.

Drake couldn't believe his ears! It was the sound of a baby crying. But that was impossible! He was all alone under the stage. He listened as the wails of the child grew louder and louder. He didn't understand who or what was making the noise, and he didn't want to find out! Terrified, Drake bolted out of the basement. He was so scared that he didn't even bother to turn off the lights on his way out.

That spooky experience was enough for Drake! After that, he steered clear of the boiler room. He did not want to encounter whatever it was that could make the sound of a crying baby.

The spirits were still active when Rebecca worked in the theater department from 2016 until 2018. She had her own strange experience in the costume room. Her job required her to spend

a considerable amount of time in the room, but she didn't like being in there.

As she would go about her tasks, she had the sense that someone—or something—was watching her. She felt a pair of unseen eyes following her every movement. The sensation sent chills down her spine.

If that wasn't scary enough, Rebecca was in the costume room one day when she heard the elevator car move to one of the upper floors. Nothing odd about that; people used the elevators all the time. When the elevator car came back downstairs, Rebecca expected someone from the theater department to walk out of the elevator when the doors opened. She was in for a shock when the doors opened, and NO ONE was there! Pretty spooky, right?!

Rebecca is sure it was a ghostly spirit who took the elevator down to the costume room to pick up a costume. What else other than a ghost could be an explanation for the elevator moving by itself? After that happened, Rebecca always made sure to say a friendly "hello" when she walked into the costume room. She wanted to be sure she did not surprise the spirit that dwells there.

Just who—or what—lingers below the stage on the University of Wisconsin-Platteville at Baraboo Sauk County campus is anyone's guess. But it seems like whatever is there isn't moving

on anytime soon. So, the next time you are at the theater, stay alert! While you are in the audience admiring the costumes on stage, a specter might be waiting in the wings for those costumes to be returned to their rightful place—the haunted costume room!

CHAPTER 5

Al. Ringling's Macabre Mansion

Would you buy a building you knew was haunted? Well, that is just what Joe Colossa did! Joe moved his family into the Al. Ringling Mansion. It is a beautiful home, and he got it for a great price. The only catch was that the building is haunted— very haunted!

Originally, the grand mansion was owned by Al. Ringling and his wife, Lou. The pair met and fell in love while performing in the circus.

Al. was an acrobat and tightrope walker, and Lou was a snake charmer. The couple got married in 1883. Before long, they stopped performing in the circus and started working behind the scenes. In time, they would run a profitable circus of their own. They became very rich and built one of the finest homes in Baraboo in 1906. And if you believe the rumors, Al. and Lou still linger in their grand home.

Joe can't say he wasn't warned about the hauntings. In 1936, the Baraboo Elks Club bought the home to host its meetings. Soon after the club moved into the building, the lodge members reported spine-tingling occurrences while they occupied the building. Some of the men saw the apparition of a young girl in the basement of the building. Others saw the ghostly figure of a woman wearing a Victorian dress on the grand staircase of the home.

The strangest event of all occurred once when a few of the men were gathered around the

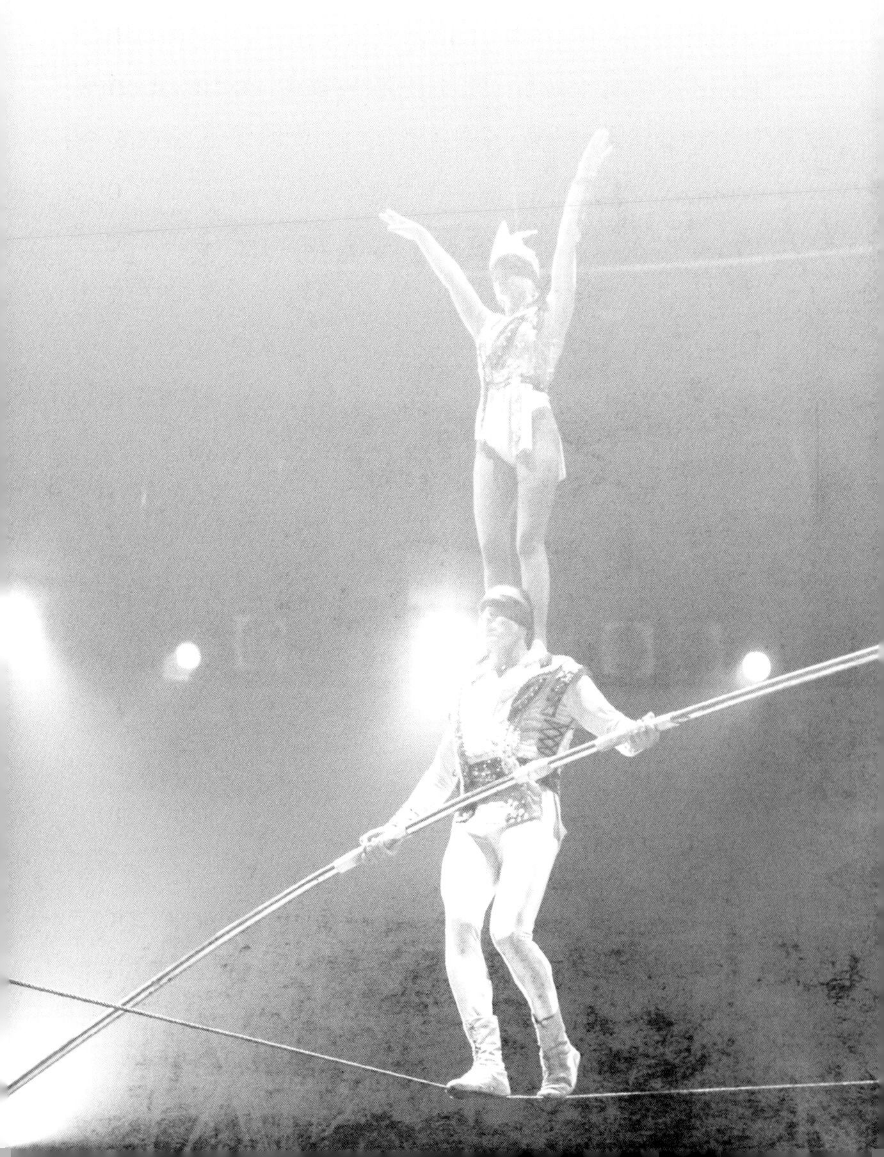

fireplace. One of the men placed a full glass of whiskey on the mantle of the fireplace. When he turned around to grab his drink, the glass was empty! Not only was the whiskey gone, but the glass had been flipped upside down. The other men swore they hadn't touched the glass. Did an unseen spirit join the men for a drink? Did it leave the glass upside down just to let the men know it was there? No one knows exactly what happened, but the men never forgot that eerie experience!

In 2013, Joe and his family moved into the Al. Ringling Mansion. They were the first family to live in the home in more than eighty years! Joe had heard all of the ghost stories, but he wasn't scared. He was used to circus people. His family had been involved in the circus for four generations. He was also used to ghosts. During his fourteen years working as a circus train master, he encountered many unusual things on the train, which was also rumored to be haunted.

He thought he would get along fine with the spirits that occupied his new home.

And he did. Shortly after he moved into the home, he was lying in bed reading one night. Suddenly, he was startled. His bed was bumped as if someone had walked into it. But there was no one in the room with him. Joe didn't panic. He set down his book and quietly told the unseen spirit that the mansion was his new home. He

explained that he wanted to be left alone while in his own space, but that the ghosts were free to roam through the other parts of the home. That seemed to work. Joe has never been bothered by ghosts in his bedroom since that day. But that doesn't mean the ghosts keep to themselves!

The ghosts make their presence known throughout the home. Joe and his wife, Carmen, often hear the sounds of ghostly footsteps climbing the grand staircase after midnight. The spirits do more than make sounds—sometimes they show themselves!

Carmen got the shock of her life when she returned home one day to see a man standing inside her house. As she approached the house, through a window, she saw a man standing in front of a mirror in her hallway. Despite being frightening, she put the key into the lock of the door, determined to enter the home.

The sound of the key in the lock startled the man. Carmen watched him run away and around the stairs inside the home. She followed the man, but he just … disappeared. She searched high and low but could not find a trace of the mysterious man. She finally realized there was a reason she could not find him. It was because the man was a ghost! And while she can't be positive, she is pretty sure that the ghost was one of the Ringling brothers!

That was not the only time the Ringlings were seen in the home. Al. Ringling, with his distinctive big, bushy mustache, was spotted in the home's foyer by Joe. The apparition was

wearing a black suit with an old-fashioned high white collar, and it looked as real as you and I do! Joe couldn't believe his eyes when the ghostly Ringling passed right through the solid front door of the home without so much as turning the doorknob!

Lou has been spotted in the home as well. One day, Joe's four-year-old daughter was standing in the doorway of the room that had belonged to Lou when she was alive. The little girl was giggling, amused by something happening in the room. Joe stood behind the girl to see what was making her laugh. Oddly, the room was empty. Joe asked the girl why she was laughing, and she said, "Lou! She is trying on dresses in the mirror, but she keeps turning around and making faces at me!" Joe took the girl's word for it even though he could not see a thing in the room!

Disembodied footsteps, unseen hands jiggling doorknobs, ghostly voices . . . this mansion has it all, and then some! If you are looking for a paranormal encounter, the Al. Ringling mansion might be the place. Ghost-seekers are in luck: the mansion is open for tours. So, you are welcome to have a look around—that is if you dare!

The AL. Ringling Theatre

The Spooky Spirits of the Ringling Theatre

Many cities across this country have haunted theaters, and Baraboo is no exception. The Al. Ringling Theatre opened its doors in 1915. If you believe the rumors, the theater has been haunted since the day it opened. The spirits that linger in the theater seem very comfortable there and show no sign of moving on anytime soon. Be forewarned, the ghastly tales from the Al. Ringling Theatre are not for the faint of heart. Read on only if you are feeling very brave.

The most famous ghost to appear in the theater is Al. Ringling himself. Generations of theatergoers have spotted him in box 17, waiting for the show to begin. It seems as if he is not just there during showtimes.

One day, a set designer brought his three-year-old daughter with him to work. There was no show in the theater that day. The building was quiet, and the seats were empty. The set designer let his little girl toddle around on her own for a bit. Before long, he found her smiling and waving. She was looking up at the box seats. (Box seats are the seats in the small balconies that circle the

theater.) The girl was looking directly at box 17.

The set designer asked his daughter what she was doing. She pointed to the center of box 17 and explained to her father that she was waving at "the man." The set designer was confused. He could not see a single person anywhere in the theater. He scanned the space, looking for someone—anyone! But the room was empty.

Concerned, her father kept a closer eye on the girl for the rest of the day. Later, the man and his daughter walked through the lobby theater on their way home. The little girl pointed to a portrait on the wall. The girl turned to her father and said, "That's the man I was waving to, Daddy!" She was pointing at a painting of Al. Ringling!

Not all the ghosts that are spotted in the theater are famous. There is a mysterious young girl who appears near the stage and an unknown boy who lingers near the pipe organ. No one knows who these youngsters are or why they are in the theater, but many have seen their ghostly forms.

The ghostly girl appears to be around twelve years old. She wears a dress with a poufy skirt, and her blonde hair is styled into ringlets. She has been spotted running along the stage so quickly she makes the stage sway with her movement. It is said she shows herself to little girls at the theater who are performing in dance recitals. The ghostly girl is said to playfully lead the young dancers into areas of the theater that they are not allowed to access.

The boy is less mischievous. He appears to be around the same age as the ghostly girl. The boy is clad in a white shirt with black suspenders and a hat. Theater employee Mary Schaefer has seen the boy many times over the years. The first time she saw him was when she was a little girl. She was in the theater watching a movie. She looked away from the screen and turned toward the organ—and saw him! The ghostly boy was sitting ABOVE the organ pipes! He had his pants rolled up to his knees, and he was dangling one leg down from his perch.

As a girl, Mary was startled to see the boy, but eventually, she forgot about him. At least, until she spotted him again when she was in high school! This time, Mary was performing on the stage of the theater. As she waited for her cue to enter the stage, she saw him again! He was backstage, watching the show. Mary and the boy looked at each other right before she entered the stage. When the show was over, Mary looked for the spooky specter, but he had vanished.

Mary encountered the boy one more time. This time, Mary was an adult and working at the concession stand of the theater. She was closing the theater one night. As she was turning off the lights, she spotted what she thought was a performer.

The person approached Mary. His mouth was moving as if he was talking. Mary could not hear anything. Slowly, the apparition faded away. It took her a few moments to realize who this figure was. It was the ghostly boy she had seen before!

But wait—there's more! This tiny tale is certain to give you goosebumps!

Have you heard about the ghostly woman in white? This wispy-looking specter wears a white dress and is often spotted in the back of the theater. Legend has it that this apparition is a mother, coming back from beyond the grave to search for her baby. The baby is rumored to have fallen from the balcony of the theater years ago. If that isn't spine-chilling enough, employees of the theater have heard the cries of the otherworldly baby this ghost is seeking! Many who work with the audio equipment during performances have reported hearing the sound of a crying baby through the sound system.

I saved the most gruesome legend for last. Read on only if you dare!

Legend has it that back in 1915 when the theater was being built, one of the workmen was injured. He severed his index finger while he was unloading steel. If you believe the tales, the finger took on a life of its own after it was cut off! This phantom finger has reportedly turned lights on and off with a flick of a switch. Most frightening, it has been blamed when an unsuspecting person in the theater receives an unexplained touch! The phantom finger continues to scuttle around the theater to this day.

It's fair to say the curtain never closes on the spooky show inside the Al. Ringling Theatre. Whether it is Al. Ringling himself, mysterious youngsters, a mournful mother, or the gruesome finger, this theater is certainly a hub of paranormal activity. Next time you are at the theater, keep your eyes wide open. The most exciting thing you see might not be what is on the stage in front of you, but the ghostly figure beside you!

CHAPTER 7

The Unseen Guest in Room One

Julie always dreamed of opening a bed and breakfast. She imagined hosting guests in a beautiful, historic mansion. The home she imagined needed to be just right. It needed to be big enough to operate a small hotel and just enough history to intrigue her visitors. When the big yellow mansion with a long front porch on Eighth Street was available for purchase, Julie was excited. It was just the type of house she was looking for!

The house is called the Charles Ringling House. It was built in 1901. Over the years, generations of the Ringling family lived in the home. The last member of the family to live in the home was Salome Juliar Ringling Clayton-Jones. Her friends called her "Sally."

While she lived in a beautiful home, Sally endured a great deal of loss during her time there. Both her grandfather and her father died of heart disease when she was young. Then, her brother died unexpectedly in a car crash. Years later, Sally's fiancé was killed in a car accident as well. Sally finally married William Clayton-Jones, a pilot. Tragically, he died in an airplane crash. Sally passed away in the home in 2005 at age 68. Her earthly body might have died, but strange happenings inside the house suggest that her spirit may still reside in the mansion.

Shortly after Julie bought the Charles Ringling House in 2015, she started to suspect that something otherworldly was happening in the home. Most of the unexplained activity occurred in Room One, the room that had been Sally's bedroom.

The first incident happened when Julie was taking a nap in Room One. She was dozing when

she felt the weight of something press into the bed. She assumed it was just her cat, joining her for a nap.

When she opened her eyes, she got quite a shock. Not only was the cat nowhere to be found, but the bedroom door was closed tight! The first time she felt the strange sensation of something joining her on the bed in Room One, she thought she might have just dreamed she felt movement on the bed. After it happened a second and then a third time, she knew something strange, maybe even supernatural, was happening in Sally's former bedroom. Could it be Sally welcoming Julie to her home?

Another time, Julie was vacuuming in Room One when the overhead light went out. She thought it was strange that every lightbulb would die at the same time. She knew it wasn't an electrical problem because her vacuum cleaner was still working. As she tried to figure out what was going on, she glanced over to the light switch in the room. It had been turned off. But how? Julie was the only person in the house at the time. Was Sally trying to get Julie's attention?

Julie was curious about Sally and any other spirits that might be in the house. She

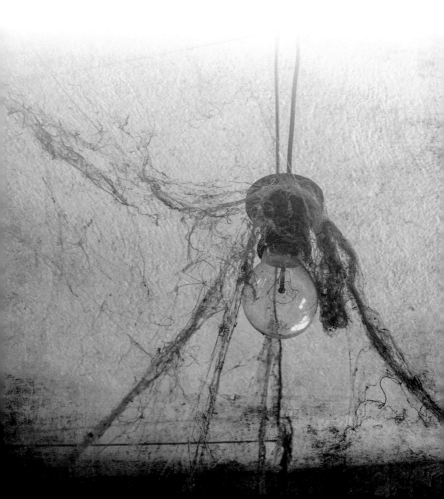

downloaded a ghost message app on her phone to communicate with the ghosts. She tried it a few times, but she didn't get much information from the app. She figured the app would not help her connect with the spirits in her home. She left the app on her phone, but she forgot about it. While Julie might have forgotten about the ghost message app, Sally apparently hadn't forgotten at all.

If Sally wanted to get Julie's attention, she got it late one night when Julie was putting laundry into a hallway closet outside of Room One. It was nearly midnight when she heard the sound of a train whistle blowing. Julie thought that was strange. The house was too far from the railroad tracks to hear the trains. She peered out the window to see where the noise was coming from when she realized the source of the sound was very close. It was in her pocket!

Her phone was making the sound of a train whistle, but that wasn't her ringtone. When she

looked down at her phone, she saw the ghost messaging app on her phone had activated itself. The ghost app had a message for her. Julie was scared. She had downloaded the app hoping to communicate with Sally. Now she had second thoughts about talking with the ghost. Was the spirit Sally? Was it safe to talk to spirits from the other side? After thinking about it, Julie decided she was too afraid to read the message. She was not sure she wanted to know what the ghost in her house wanted to say to her. She never opened the message.

One of Sally's old friends visited the bed and breakfast shortly after it was opened. Julie told her about the strange things that she experienced in Room One. Julie asked Sally's friend if perhaps these unexplained events were Sally trying to communicate with her. The friend said, "Well, if anyone could do it, Sally could."

Could it be that Sally still resides in her former home? If it is her, why does she stay in

the Charles Ringling House? Guests who stay in Room One have reported feeling someone—or something—sitting on the bed in the middle of the night. Would that be enough to keep you away from Room One? Or would you welcome a late-night visit from Sally?

St. Mary's Ringling Hospital

Ask anyone in Baraboo what the town's most haunted building is, and chances are they'll say it is the abandoned hospital on Tenth Street. The dilapidated building, with its broken windows and moldy walls, looks exactly the way you'd imagine a haunted building to look. Over the years, the building has been many things: a private residence, a hospital, a nursing home, and a convent. From 1922 to 1959, it was St.

Mary's Ringling Hospital, with twenty-five beds available to patients, but it has been vacant for more than twenty years. That is unless you count the ghosts that call the deserted building their home.

Neighbors claim to hear eerie noises coming from the supposedly empty building. Some have reported lights shining from inside the former hospital—despite the fact that the electricity at the property was shut off years ago. The building has been empty since 1998, but the sights and sounds of something roaming inside the creepy building continue.

All of these strange reports caught the attention of ghost hunters. In 2011, the Paranormal Investigators of Sauk County (PISC), headed by Tom Dyar, decided to investigate the building. The team spent three days in the abandoned hospital. They figured it would take that long for the ghosts to feel comfortable enough to communicate with the investigators.

The crew found plenty of evidence that something still lingered in the supposedly abandoned building! As they walked through the former hospital for the first time, their equipment

recorded unexplained shadows and captured strange sounds—and that was just the beginning! The longer they remained in the building, the eerier the investigation became.

Over the next three days, the group witnessed a small, dark image scurrying across the floors. When they aimed their flashlights at the shadowy figure, there was nothing there. Another time, they heard footsteps and the sounds of voices behind them as they walked down a dark hallway. But when they turned around to investigate the sounds, there was no one there. At least no one they could see.

Once, the ghost hunters were certain they heard a cheerful, but disembodied voice asking, "Well, how are you?" Who uttered those words? Maybe it was the apparition of a nurse from long ago that repeatedly showed up in the photographs the team captured during the investigation?

In one of the images the team captured, it looked as if the ghostly figure was wearing a nurse uniform from the hospital was first opened and holding a clipboard. Another image caught a figure wearing the same type of outfit holding a baby. Is this voice and are these photographs evidence that a nurse, or maybe many nurses, continue to work in the old hospital long past their earthly lives?

The investigators found the room directly behind the old chapel in the hospital to be the room with the most spirit activity. While using a voice recorder, Tom Dyar tried to get the spirits in the room to communicate with him by using two flashlights. He placed the flashlights on a table and then asked the spirits questions that could be answered with a simple "yes," or "no." He asked the spirits to turn on the purple flashlight if they wanted to answer yes to one of his questions. If the light on the black flashlight turned on, that meant the answer to the question was no.

Before long, the flashlights

began to turn on and off without anyone touching them! Tom wanted to know why the ghosts were in the building. He asked the unseen spirits in the room if they were trapped in the old hospital. The black flashlight lit up! They weren't trapped. Tom believes the spirits he connected with still linger in the building for two reasons. For some of the spirits, the hospital is the last place they remember being alive, and so it is where they remain. For others, they spent so much time in the hospital while they were living, they decided to continue to visit the building from beyond the grave.

Many ghost hunters believe that ghosts are most active around three in the morning. And it appears that the spirits linger in the old hospital prove that to be true. On the final night of the investigation, at three in the morning, the generator the investigators were using to light the abandoned building ran out of power and died. The investigators were on the third floor of the building when they were plunged into darkness!

The ghost hunters had flashlights, but every investigator who attempted to turn on their flashlight found the batteries inside were dead. They were trapped in the dark! Slowly, they tried to make their way out of the spooky building. They took small steps and felt their way along the walls to try to find an exit.

Without warning, a bright, volleyball-sized orb flashed out of the ceiling! Orbs are strange balls of light. People can see them but can't explain where they come from. Lots of people think they are a sign that a spirit is present. Orbs can be any size, even as small as a tiny fly. A volleyball-sized orb is rare and HUGE!

The orb lit up the dark hallway as if it were a lamp. The stunned ghost hunters watched in awe as the glowing orb slowly floated toward them. The orb stopped at each open door in the dark hallway. Later, the investigators would say the movement of the orb reminded them of a nurse checking in on patients.

If this wasn't scary enough, what happened next is unbelievable! The glowing orb got closer to the ghost hunters. Before it reached them, it suddenly transformed into a mist! The mist rushed toward the investigators. One described the mist as looking like a "bear with ghostlike arms." To the investigators, it seemed like the mist was trying to get them to leave the building. After that, the group fled the abandoned hospital as quickly as they could.

All of the strange happenings that occurred during the three-day investigation left the team with more questions than answers.

One final, haunting question sends shivers up the spines of those who live in the neighborhood: what will become of the ghosts who have made the abandoned hospital their home when the building is torn down? Will they disappear as the pile of rubble that was once the hospital is hauled away? Or, as many fear, will the spirits simply move into the nearby homes?

Once the old hospital is finally torn down, a nighttime walk through the neighborhood might reveal what happened to all of those ghosts. Will you feel cold shivers up your spine as you walk along the sidewalk? Maybe catch a shadow figure glide by out of the corner of your eye? Only time will tell what happens to these ghosts. Will you be brave enough to find out?!

CHAPTER 9

The Phantom of First Street

"Puppies get into everything!" Martin Green thought to himself as he cleaned up the plants that were knocked onto the floor of his new apartment. He had just moved into the apartment on First Street with his wife and his two-month-old black Lab mix puppy. They had moved so Martin could start his new job teaching science at the local high school.

As he swept up the dirt on the floor, Martin wondered how his puppy managed to get out of the kitchen while he was at school. When they first moved in, he put a baby gate in front of the kitchen door to keep her in the tiled room when she was home alone. But this wasn't the first time she escaped.

The first time he had left his puppy alone, when he returned home he found her napping on the sofa in the living room. The gate hadn't been knocked over; however, it didn't seem possible for such a small dog to jump over the gate. So, Martin stacked TWO baby gates in the doorway to keep the puppy in the kitchen. The two gates created a barrier that was almost as tall as he was! He looked at it and thought there was no way the puppy would be able to get out of the kitchen now!

Imagine how surprised he was when he got home that day and saw the puppy on the couch— again! And this time, the dog had knocked over several of the plants in the living room. How did the puppy manage to get over the tall gate? How was it able to reach the plants on the table in the living room? The science teacher was puzzled. He knew there must be a rational explanation for what happened. But what was it?

In time, the only explanation that made sense was that there was a ghost was in the house!

When the dog got a little older, the Greens bought the dog a plastic kennel. The dog spent her days in the kennel while Martin and his wife were at work. The black Lab mix quickly got used to the kennel. She seemed to enjoy being in it and would often nap in the cozy spot when the Greens were at home.

One day, Martin got home from work and was surprised to find the dog loose inside the house. Martin went to the kennel to see how the dog got out. He was shocked and a little frightened by what he saw. He saw someone or

something had cut a small triangle in the upper right side of the kennel.

Martin was sure the hole had been cut. There were no signs of chewing or teeth marks around the hole in the crate. The dog could not have made the hole. It wasn't Martin or his wife. No one else had keys to the apartment. So, who did it? Martin wasn't sure, but the whole thing made him feel uneasy.

Sometime later, the person who lived in the apartment before the Green family visited the building. Martin told her about the puppy getting out of the kitchen and the hole in the kennel. She wasn't surprised to hear of the unexplained events that occurred in the building. Strange things happened to her and her animals when she lived there, too.

While living in the apartment, she did some investigating to see if she could understand what was happening inside the building. She discovered that an elderly man died in the building years ago. Could his spirit be behind all the strange occurrences in the apartment?

Even though Martin now knew what might be causing these unusual happenings in the apartment, they didn't stop. But it did make him much more curious to try to uncover the truth about whether or not a ghost was living with him and his wife.

So he did some investigating of his own. He wondered if the source of the supernatural activity might be in the building's attic. So, he hauled out his ladder and decided to it check out.

Martin climbed the ladder until he was able to reach the small trap door in the ceiling that led to the attic. He pushed on the door, but it would not budge. He pushed on it again, this time using all the strength he could muster. He still could not get the door open. It seemed to be sealed tight. Martin soon gave up trying to get into the attic. He put his ladder away and soon forgot about the whole thing.

That is, until a few nights later. Martin and his wife were fast asleep when they were startled awake by the sound of a loud bang. Martin leaped out of bed and sprung to his feet. The bang caused him to think someone must have broken into the apartment. He grabbed a nearby baseball bat and crept down the hall, in search of the source of the racket.

He checked the front and back doors but found them locked. He even searched the basement. No one was there. Martin was certain the bang came from inside the house. He looked into the

doorway of each room. At last, he found the source of the noise.

There, on the floor, was the small hatch door that led to the attic. It had, somehow, fallen from the ceiling. Martin was confused. He could not understand how this door, which was sealed tight just days earlier, opened itself. When he attempted to replace the doorway to the attic, he was even more confused.

Martin could not slide the hatch back into the ceiling. He was forced to place the panel in diagonally and then straighten the panel once it was inside the attic in order to close it. It was the only way he could get the hatch to fit into the attic. Martin thought it was impossible for the panel to fall out of the ceiling. It needed someone or something to turn the panel before it could be removed. Who—or what—made the panel fall from the ceiling? Was it the ghost of the old man the former tenant told him about?

Maybe the mystery of who was behind all of

these unexplained happenings in the apartment was revealed on the day Martin and his family moved out of the building. After Martin loaded the final box into the moving truck, he turned back to look at the empty apartment one last time.

That was when Martin spotted him! He saw a man standing at the upper bedroom window! The man was peeking out from behind the Venetian blinds. The man was hidden, except for his eyebrows, nose, and the fingers that held the blinds open. But Martin didn't need to see anymore. He was just relieved to finally leave the apartment—and the spirit that haunted the place—for good.

Martin might have moved out of the apartment, but there is evidence that the spirit remained. In the years after the Green family left, tenants would report flickering lights and switches that would shut themselves on and off. Disembodied footsteps could be heard walking through the empty upper floor. Children's toys

would turn on and make noises, despite not having any batteries in them.

And that is just a few of the things that happened. The restless spirit did not stop making itself known to the living. Each new family that moved into the strange apartment had their own spine-tingling tales to tell of their time in the home.

With all of the eerie events that have happened, odds are good that apartment is vacant and waiting for new tenants. Could that be you and your family? Would you dare to move in with the spooky spirit they call the Phantom of First Street?

CHAPTER
10

The Mysterious Highway 12 Hitchhiker

You've probably been warned countless times to never pick up a hitchhiker. It is just too dangerous to allow a stranger into your car. In Baraboo, drivers are cautioned against hitchhikers—both the living and the undead!

There is a stretch of Highway 12 that runs between Lake Delton and Baraboo that is famous throughout Wisconsin, or perhaps infamous is a bit more accurate. It is on that stretch of road that people claim to see a ghostly hitchhiker. No one knows just who he is, but he's been seen so many times on lonely stretches of Highway 12 that few deny his existence.

For years, he has been seen walking along the side of the road in a green Army jacket. He wears a hat atop his dark, shoulder-length hair, and he carries a backpack. The hitchhiker is always seen from behind, walking in the same direction as the cars that are speeding along Highway 12. He walks very close to the edge of the road—dangerously close! Many drivers have swerved over the center lane of the road to avoid hitting this ghostly figure.

Those who drive past the mysterious man turn their heads as they drive past, hoping to see his face, but they never catch a glimpse of him. Sometimes, it is a heavy fog that obscures his features. Other times the man is cloaked in the darkness of night as headlights move past him. It could be the speed of the car, the poorly timed turn of the head to look at him. Whatever it may be, there is always SOMETHING that keeps his face hidden.

So far, nothing scary, right? So, what? It's just a guy walking alongside a highway. I'm sure that is what most drivers think when they pass him alongside Highway 12—at least, the FIRST time they pass him.

Imagine, you are in a car that passes the man. You are startled to see someone walking along the roadside, but you would likely forget about him in a few minutes as you continue to cruise down Highway 12. Then, you spot something up ahead, on the right side of the road. As your car gets closer, the object comes into focus. You see the green Army jacket and then the backpack. You can't believe it! It is the man you passed just a few minutes ago! How is the man ahead of your car again?! It is impossible

for him to walk faster than your car is driving, but there he is.

There must be a logical explanation, right?

That is just what a group of friends thought when they decided to go for a drive on Highway 12 to search for this mysterious apparition. It was a foggy night when Jacob Carignan and three of his buddies loaded into Jacob's old car.

Mist curled at the windows of the car as Jacob told his friends the legend of the Highway 12 hitchhiker. Rather than being frightened, his friends laughed. They were confident that ghosts did not exist. The guys joked as they pressed down the door locks of Jacob's car "to keep the ghosts out."

They weren't laughing for long.

The car's headlights broke through the fog as they drove down Highway 12. Jacob saw something ahead on the side of the road but thought it might be an animal. As the car got closer to the figure on the side of the road, Jacob could see it was no animal. All it took was a flash of the green Army coat for Jacob to know what was ahead. Suddenly, one of the friends shrieked in terror! The earlier laughter turned into fear. There he was—the Highway 12 hitchhiker! As the car swerved around the hitchhiker, the boys turned to look at the man's face. But, true to the legend, he was just a blur as they drove by him.

Frightened, the friends continued to travel down Highway 12 until they reached a dead end. They were unsure about what to do. They needed to turn around and go back the way they came to get home. But that meant they had to pass the mysterious hitchhiker again. It was too scary to even imagine driving by him a second time!

As they sat in the car and debated over what to do, all of the sudden, the car doors unlocked by themselves all at once! The car did not have automatic locks, and there was no way for this to happen. Well, at least no way any of the living beings in the car could have made the doors unlock. But maybe it is something a ghost could do!

In a flash, the guys decided to get out of there before the Highway 12 hitchhiker showed himself again. They drove as quickly as they could toward home and away from the strange spirit that lingers on that lonely stretch of road.

The next time you are driving down Highway 12, be on the lookout for a figure on the side of the road or a flash of Army green in the rearview mirror. You never know when the legendary Highway 12 hitchhiker will appear. Or reappear!

Anna Lardinois tingles the spines of Milwaukee locals and visitors through her haunted, historical walking tours known as Gothic Milwaukee. The former English teacher is an ardent collector of stories, an avid walker and a sweet treat enthusiast. She happily resides in a historic home in Milwaukee that, at this time, does not appear to be haunted.

Check out some of the other Spooky America titles available now!

Spooky America was adapted from the creeptastic Haunted America series for adults. Haunted America explores historical haunts in cities and regions across America. Each book chronicles both the widely known and less-familiar history behind local ghosts and other unexplained mysteries. Here's more from *Haunted Baraboo* authors Shelley Mordini and Gwen Herrewig: